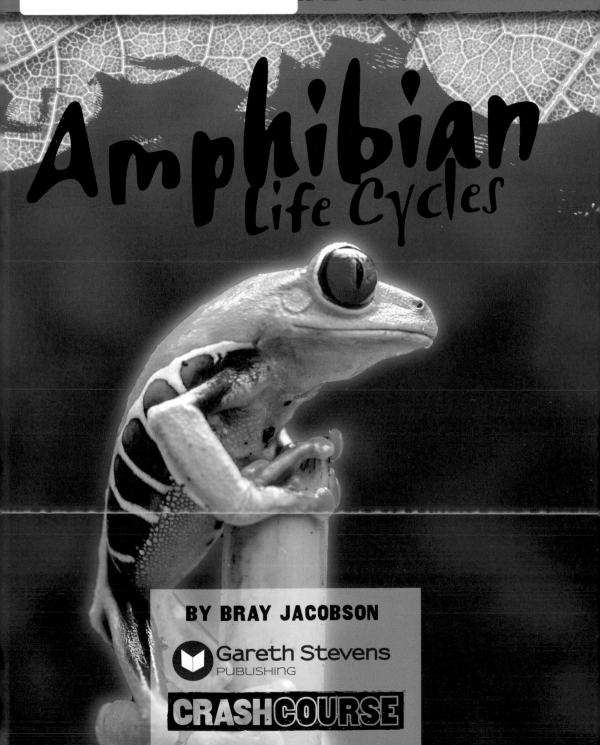

Amphibian Life Cycles

BY BRAY JACOBSON

Gareth Stevens
PUBLISHING

CRASHCOURSE

Please visit our website, www.garethstevens.com. For a free color catalog of all our high-quality books, call toll free 1-800-542-2595 or fax 1-877-542-2596.

Cataloging-in-Publication Data
Names: Jacobson, Bray.
Title: Amphibian life cycles / Bray Jacobson.
Description: New York : Gareth Stevens Publishing, 2018. | Series: A look at life cycles | Includes index.
Identifiers: ISBN 9781538210352 (pbk.) | ISBN 9781538210338 (library bound) | ISBN 9781538210321 (6 pack)
Subjects: LCSH: Frogs--Life cycles--Juvenile literature.
Classification: LCC QL668.E2 J25 2018 | DDC 597.8'9--dc23

First Edition

Published in 2018 by
Gareth Stevens Publishing
111 East 14th Street, Suite 349
New York, NY 10003

Designer: Samantha DeMartin
Editor: Kristen Nelson

Photo credits: Series art Im stocker/Shutterstock.com; cover, p. 1 Kobby Dagan/Shutterstock.com; p. 5 Serhii Fedoruk/Shutterstock.com; p. 7 (toad) Hurly D'souza/Shutterstock.com; p. 7 (caecilian) reptiles4all/Shutterstock.com; p. 7 (salamander) Beatrice Prezzemoli/Shutterstock.com; p. 7 (frog) Alen thien/Shutterstock.com; p. 7 (newt) Bildagentur Zonar GmbH/Shutterstock.com; p. 9 (salamander) DEA/A. PETRETTI/De Agostini/Getty Images; p. 9 (salamander larva) De Agostini Picture Library/De Agostini/Getty Images; p. 11 SidBradypus/Shutterstock.com; p. 13 PusitGuru/Shutterstock.com; p. 15 (frog) Olhastock/Shutterstock.com; p. 15 (frog illustration) snapgalleria/Shutterstock.com; p. 17 E R DEGGINGER/Science Source/Getty Images; p. 19 SCOTT CAMAZINE/Science Source/Getty Images; p. 21 cristi180884/Shutterstock.com; p. 23 (newt) Tiberiu Sahlean/Shutterstock.com; p. 23 (newt eft) Jay Ondreicka/Shutterstock.com; p. 25 Dante Fenolio/Science Source/Getty Images; pp. 27 (main), 29 Michael & Patricia Fogden/Minden Pictures/Getty Images; p. 27 (inset) JAMES HANKEN/Science Source/Getty Images; p. 30 kamnuan/Shutterstock.com.

Printed in the United States of America

CPSIA compliance information: Batch #CW18GS: For further information contact Gareth Stevens, New York, New York at 1-800-542-2595.

Contents

What Makes an Amphibian?   4

A Big Change   8

Frog Life   10

The Amazing Salamander   16

Don't Forget Newts!   22

The Caecilian   24

Caecilian Life Cycle   30

Glossary   31

For More Information   32

Index   32

Words in the glossary appear in **bold** type the first time they are used in the text.

What Makes an Amphibian?

Amphibians are one of the main groups of animals found on Earth. Amphibians live part of their life in water and part on land. Their skin is moist, or wet. They often live near water to stay this way!

Make the Grade

Amphibians are vertebrates, which means they have a backbone.

The amphibian group is made up of many **diverse** animals. Frogs and toads are amphibians. So are salamanders and newts. There's another group of amphibians called caecilians (sih-SIHL-yuhnz). They look like big worms!

Make the Grade

Most caecilians don't have legs or arms, have very small eyes, and have body parts called tentacles (TEHN-tuh-kuhlz) used for sensing.

caecilian

toad

salamander

newt

frog

A Big Change

The different groups of amphibians have parts of their **life cycles** that are alike. First, many amphibian **species** lay eggs. It's also common for amphibians to have **aquatic** larvae that don't look much like adults. Let's take a look at some amphibian life cycles!

Make the Grade

The changes an amphibian larva goes through to become an adult is called metamorphosis (meh-tuh-MOHR-fuh-suhs).

salamander

salamander
larva

Frog Life

All frogs **hatch** from eggs. Female frogs lay a huge mass of eggs, commonly on the water or in moist places. There may be thousands of eggs in one egg mass! An egg mass looks a little like a tiny bunch of grapes.

Make the Grade

Toads have a similar life cycle to frogs. But toads lay their eggs in a chain rather than a mass.

After a few days or weeks, most frogs hatch as tadpoles. Tadpoles are larvae that have tails and **gills** for living in the water. It takes a lot of food for them to grow. They eat **algae**, plants, and sometimes even other tadpoles!

Make the Grade

How long it takes for a tadpole to grow legs and become a frog depends on the species. It could be a few weeks or a few months!

13

Once a tadpole has grown legs, it starts to lose its tail and gills and grows **lungs** so it can breathe air. Now called a froglet, it will move from water to land. Its body changes so it can start to eat like an adult frog, too!

Make the Grade

Adult frogs eat many different bugs, including flies, moths, and even grasshoppers!

Frog
Life Cycle

Eggs are laid by the female frog.

Frog embryos grow a tail while still inside the egg.

Tadpoles breathe through gills, start to grow legs, and have a tail.

Froglets have all four legs. Their tail starts to get shorter.

Adult frogs breathe air, have four legs, and no tail.

The Amazing Salamander

Salamanders commonly **mate** in the spring. Most kinds then lay eggs. Female salamanders carry eggs in their body for just a few days. Most salamander species lay their eggs in water. Mother salamanders often lay about 100 eggs at a time.

Make the Grade

Salamander eggs are like little balls of jelly!

17

Salamanders hatch after about a month. The larvae have a tail and are good swimmers. They hunt for tiny water animals to eat as soon as they hatch! Salamander larvae have gills to breathe underwater.

Make the Grade

Some salamanders lay their eggs on land. Others have eggs that **develop** and hatch inside the mother's body!

19

Not long after they hatch, salamander larvae start to grow legs. After about 2 months, salamanders begin looking like adults. They've grown four legs and lost their gills and tail fins. It takes about 2 years to be fully grown, though.

Make the Grade

Fire salamanders give birth to live young! They may have as many as 30 babies at a time.

Salamander
Life Cycle

Adult salamanders mate.

Female salamanders lay eggs.

Larvae hatch and hunt underwater.

Young salamanders lose their tail fins, gills, and look like small adults.

Larvae grow legs.

Don't Forget Newts!

The newt is a kind of salamander. Its life cycle is very much the same as other salamanders! However, some newts don't spend much time in water as larvae. Instead, they live as larvae on land. In this part of their life cycle, they're called efts.

Make the Grade

All newts are salamanders, but not all salamanders are newts!

23

The Caecilian

There are about 200 species of caecilians. Some kinds lay eggs and have a life cycle similar to that of other amphibians. But about 75 percent give birth to live young! These baby caecilians are born fully developed.

Make the Grade

Caecilians that hatch from eggs live in water as larvae, just as frogs, toads, and many salamanders do.

25

Many young caecilians stay with their mother for several weeks after they're born. Their mother grows a special thick, fatty layer of skin her babies feed on during this time. Some young caecilians have special teeth for this!

Make the Grade

In order to peel off their mother's skin to eat, young caecilians have short, dull teeth as well as long, hooklike teeth.

X-ray showing caecilian teeth

27

Whether born as eggs or live young, most caecilians tunnel underground—and stay there! A few kinds of caecilians in South America do live in water, though. It's unlikely you'll ever see one!

Make the Grade

There's a lot scientists still don't know about caecilians, including how they live underground and find mates.

29

Caecilian
Life Cycle

Live Young: Baby caecilians grow inside their mother.

Live Young: Caecilian mothers give birth to live young.

Eggs: Mother caecilians lay eggs near water.

Eggs: Caecilian larvae hatch with gills and finned tails.

Caecilians mate.

Live Young: The babies stay with their mother and eat her skin.

Caecilians tunnel underground.

Eggs: Caecilian young grow a lung, thicker skin, and sensing parts.

30

Glossary

algae: plantlike living things that are mostly found in water

aquatic: living, growing, or spending time in water

develop: to grow and change

diverse: differing from each other

gill: the body part that animals such as fish use to breathe in water

hatch: to break open or come out of

life cycle: the stages through which a living thing passes in its life

lung: a sack-like body part that a land animal uses to breathe

mate: to come together to make babies. Also, one of two animals that come together to make babies.

species: a group of plants or animals that are all the same kind

For More Information

Books

Amstutz, L. J. *Investigating Animal Life Cycles*. Minneapolis, MN: Lerner Publications, 2016.

Berne, Emma Carlson. *Amphibians*. North Mankato, MN: Capstone Press, 2017.

Websites

Amphibians

kids.sandiegozoo.org/animals/amphibians

Learn more about amphibians, and find links to information about other kinds of animals.

Publisher's note to educators and parents: Our editors have carefully reviewed these websites to ensure that they are suitable for students. Many websites change frequently, however, and we cannot guarantee that a site's future contents will continue to meet our high standards of quality and educational value. Be advised that students should be closely supervised whenever they access the Internet.

Index

adults 8, 14, 15, 20, 21

caecilians 6, 24, 26, 28, 30

eft 22

eggs 8, 10, 15, 16, 18, 21, 24, 28, 30

frogs 6, 10, 12, 14, 15, 24

gills 12, 14, 15, 18, 20, 21, 30

larvae 8, 12, 18, 20, 21, 22, 24, 30

legs 6, 12, 14, 15, 20, 21,

live young 20, 24, 28, 30

lungs 14, 30

metamorphosis 8

newts 6, 22

salamanders 6, 16, 18, 20, 21, 22, 24

tadpoles 12, 15

tail 12, 14, 15, 18, 20, 21, 30

teeth 26

toads 6, 10, 24